BORN OF ASHES:
WOODFIRED CERAMICS

Catalogue and Introduction by
Alan Du Bois

The Arkansas Arts Center Decorative Arts Museum
January 10 - February 21, 1999

The Arkansas Arts Center
Decorative Arts Museum
East Seventh and Rock Streets
P.O. Box 2137
Little Rock, AR 72203-2137

Telephone: (501)372-4000
Fax: (501)375-8053
E-mail: center@arkarts.org

Director and Chief Curator: Townsend Wolfe
Curator of Decorative Arts: Alan Du Bois
Curatorial Assistant: Christine Laba
Editor: Michael Preble

Acknowledgements:
This catalogue has been underwritten by John and Robyn Horn
to whom the museum and the artists represented wish to express
their heartfelt gratitude and appreciation.

Season Sponsors:
Beverly Enterprises; Ernst & Young LLP; Giroir, Gregory, Holmes & Hoover, PLC

Photography by:
Cindy Momchilov, Camera Work Inc., Little Rock, Arkansas

Front cover: (detail) JAR by Don Reitz
Back cover: (detail) JAR FORM WITH PARALLEL STROKES (94J) by Paul Chaleff

Editorial Note:
All dimensions are given in inches; height precedes width and depth.

Printed in the U.S.A. by Davco Graphics, Little Rock, Arkansas

ISBN 1-884240-19-4

Contents

Introduction

Born of Ashes is an exhibition of contemporary ceramic ware that, in addition to being formed by hand, is transformed by a torrent of fire and ash in a wood-burning kiln. The content of each piece tends to be "autobiographical," that is, each pot has its own "narrative" that tells about its encounter with the fire. Colors range over a surprisingly wide, but harmonious, palette from a delicate blush caused by "flashing" to more intense variations of earth tones — red, yellow, blue, green, gray and black. "Hot" and "cold" spots document forever the flow of the fire. Brighter colors are revealed on the clay body facing the fire. Pale, subtle colors are on surfaces facing away from the fire. Deposits of falling ash resemble a textured salt and pepper dusting on upper exposed surfaces and melted runs follow a gravitational flow. Textures can be smooth or distressed with blistered surfaces that remind us of fire-formed igneous rock. The process and the effect suggests a strong and timeless kinship with the primordial forces of nature.

Woodfired clay has a long history; evidence of its use has been found in pre-historic shards. By the sixth century, technology in Asia had advanced to a point where potters could achieve and sustain temperatures high enough to fire stoneware and porcelain, a feat not duplicated in Europe until early in the eighteenth century. Tunnel kilns burrowing into the sides of mountains were developed in Korea and China and eventually spread to Japan, where they are called *anagama* kilns - meaning "hole" or "cave." Later, a climbing multi-chambered kiln, called *noborigama* was developed. It had arched chambers at right angles to the air flow allowing improved temperature control. These kilns became nearly obsolete in the seventeenth century when changing tastes, production technology for foreign trade and more efficient fuels were introduced. In Europe, and eventually in America, box, catenary, and bottle-type kilns were the rule through the early-twentieth century. An exception is the shallow arched "ground hog" kiln utilized in North Carolina.

A curious development occurred in Japan in the late-sixteenth and early-seventeenth centuries when connoisseurs of the tea ceremony admired and demanded the simple, natural and humble pottery from woodfired kilns. The admiration of urban sophisticates for country pottery and an increased sensibility and love for nature elevated the status of woodfired pottery to a fine art. In the 1920s and 1930s, this admiration was rekindled by persons who sought to preserve the historic past and folk traditions that were fast disappearing in the rush to embrace the industrial revolution. This was the genesis of the *Mingei,* or folk craft movement, in Japan.

With the exception of a brief flirtation with Japanese art by Rookwood and other art potteries at the end of the nineteenth century, American potters drew their inspiration from Europe until the 1950s. Then, a pivotal point came when Bernard Leach, an English potter who studied ceramics in Japan from 1910-1920 melded ideas of the East (Zen Buddhism) and West (arts and craft movement) with Shoji Hamada, a Japanese potter, and Soetsu Yanagi, founder of the *Mingei* movement. These three men shared their ideas in two transcontinental tours that included Black Mountain College, North Carolina; Minneapolis, Minnesota; Archie Bray Foundation, Helena, Montana and Mills College, California. This new aesthetic offered an alternative to the mechanical precision of European form and opened up expressive routes that corresponded to mainstream art — surrealiam and abstract expressionism. These routes included finding beauty in imperfection, embracing the accident and the element of chance, as well as giving form asymmetry, movement, gesture and tactile surfaces. A number of potters in this exhibition have traveled and studied in Asia and Japan. They are Rob Barnard, Paul Chaleff, Randy James Johnston, Will Ruggles and Jeff Shapiro. Others, like Joe Bruhin, Chuck Hindes, Douglass Rankin, Jan McKeachie-Johnston, John Skelton and Jack Troy, while not having traveled to Asia, give an aesthetic nod in that direction. Jack Troy points out that there are those like Mark Hewitt, Peg Malloy, Skeff Thomas and Jane Shellenbarger, who are making woodfired pottery in the European tradition and, finally, potters like Dan Anderson, Peter Callas, John Balistreri, Karen Karnes, Maren Kloppmann and Graham Marks who appear to be working out an independent aesthetic of their own.

Many potters have told the story that the process of woodfiring has a certain rhythm. Some fire once or twice a year others, more often. Woodfiring involves a period of preparation in which wood is gathered, dried and split, and the clay prepared. Next, there is the phase of creation in which the forms are thrown, built and embellished. Transformation follows when the kiln is loaded and the firing takes place. Finally, rest and introspection often occurs while the kiln cools, and when the kiln is opened and the work inspected.

The variables in firing a woodfired kiln are many. They include the type, size, and length of wood used, its moisture content, the character of the clay and slips, how and where the works are stacked in the kiln, the flow of the flame, the rise of temperature, the length of time at various temperatures, the amount of ash, the amount of oxidation or reduction of the fire, the outside atmosphere, and even ground chemicals and moisture content. The process involves control in the making of the work and the willingness to give up control to the firing. Woodfire potters are invigorated by accidents and surprise, and speak of each firing as a learning experience. They live on the edge somewhere between purgatory and paradise.

With firings lasting up to nine days, it is clear that the process is often a communal undertaking. Fellow potters and friends bring unfired pots, firewood, food, tents, campers and sleeping bags. All are organized into teams and shifts to fire the kiln, while others supply food and encouragement. The round-the-clock effort is analogous to the intense time of gathering in the harvest. It is not unusual, then, to see many of the artists here have fired their work in another artist's kiln. For example, Peter Voulkos has fired his work in Peter Callas' anagama kiln in New Jersey. Robert Archambeau and Don Reitz fire in Dan Anderson's "Mounds" anagama in Edwardsville, Illinois. Archambeau, who lives in Canada, fires with John Neely in Logan, Utah; Chuck Hindes in Iowa City; and Torbjorn Kvasbo in Venabygd, Norway.

Perhaps Jack Troy best sums up the woodfire process in his essay "No Ideas, But in Things" appearing in the exhibition catalogue for *American Woodfire '91*, "Occasionally one gets a sense of a cosmic blessing emanating from woodfired work - the feeling that everything and everyone was in the right place and at the right time, and the only way to prove this improbable conjecture is the existence of the work itself. Encounters between matter and spirit, the linking of human with non-human forces - the interface between consciousness and chance."

ADB

Suggested Reading:

Conklin, Jo-Ann and Chuck Hindes. *American Woodfire '91*, exhibition catalogue with essays "No Ideas, But in Things" by Jack Troy and "Between to Fires" by Randy James Johnston. Iowa City: The University of Iowa Museum of Art, 1991.

Ferrin, Leslie. *A Wealth of Woodfiring*, exhibition catalogue. Northhampton, MA: Ferrin Gallery, 1998.

Lopez, Barry. "Before the Temple of Fire." *Harper's Magazine* (January 1998): 35-50.

Hansen, Steve. "Women Who Fire with Wood." *Ceramics Monthly,* 46:8 (October 1998): 45-49.

Millard, Charles. *Mark Hewitt: Potter*, exhibition catalogue with contributions by Sherman Lee, Charlotte Brown, Louise Allison Cort, Charles Zug and Mark Hewitt. Raleigh: Foundation Gallery, Visual Arts Center, North Carolina State University, 1997.

Troy, Jack. *Wood-Fired Stoneware and Porcelain*. Radnot, PA: Chilton Book Co., 1995.

Williams, Gerry, "The Japanese Pottery Tradition and Its Influence on American Ceramics." *American Craft,* April/May 1998: 52-59, 79.

Catalogue

Dan Anderson

American, born 1945

"My artwork, an amalgam of vessel and industrial artifact, is full of irony - handmade replicas of manmade objects, soft clay renderings of metal objects, aged and impotent reminders of a once powerful age. The oil and gasoline cans represent the machinery that once threatened to devalue the work of human beings. Now they seem just like the hardworking humans they served - stoic, dignified, straightforward, but plumb wore out.

The usefulness of machines in their original states is limited - as the products of progress, they are doomed to obsolescence - but by recreating them in a "primitive" medium, I believe they will endure through the ages. They have been transformed for eternity into art. In this way, too, I have taken the aesthetic and political ugliness out of industry, reminding everyone that change can be both hurtful/traumatic and positive/healing. Once again underscoring the power of art to uplift the human condition.

By firing the oil and gas cans in my anagama kiln, I am convinced that instead of merely heating the clay, the flame and ash have the capacity to alter and enhance my clay cans. The etched surface, created by sustained three to five day firing, imbues a "poetic" richness. What an interesting conspiracy: man/woman, clay and fire."

1. **Gas Can**, 1998
   stoneware, wire; woodfired in the artist's "Mounds" anagama kiln
   10 x 8 x 10"

2. **·Oval Gas Can**, 1998
   stoneware, wire; woodfired in the artist's "Mounds" anagama kiln
   25 x 15 x 7"
   The Arkansas Arts Center Foundation Collection

3. **Gas Can**, 1998
   stoneware, wire; woodfired in the artist's "Mounds" anagama kiln
   13 x 12 x 9"
   Collection of John and Robyn Horn, Little Rock, Arkansas

1.

3.

2.

Robert Archambeau

American, born 1933

"My goal would be to continue developing those aspects of my work which I am currently involved in but MORE, BIGGER AND BETTER. Most of my ceramic work, for the past fifteen years, has been woodfired. Woodfiring is difficult, expensive and labor intensive. A more prudent and less compulsive artist might consider it not worth the effort to fire with wood, but the total aesthetic is what I am after and woodfiring is the only way to achieve it. Woodfiring is very often a shared activity. Over the past ten years I have worked with Dan Anderson, Chuck Hindes, John Neely and Torbjorn Kvasbo, all internationally known artists with long experience in woodfiring. Each

of their respective kilns yield results quite particular to the type of basic structure of their kiln, the type(s) of wood burned and the idiosyncrasies and firing technique of the owners. Torbjorn Kvasbo's kiln located in Venabygd, Norway gives firing results that have an extraordinary range of color; light auburns flash to pinks and beige, black-browns grey into deep purple.

I have worked closely with Dan Anderson the past three years. His anagama wood kiln in Edwardsville, Illinois, is well known and a veritable mecca for potters from all over North America. He is quite knowledgeable regarding woodfiring and very altruistic with his large kiln

and all that he has learned from firing over several years. It is a 2,500 mile round-trip for me to fire with Dan, but I always have a productive time and find it well worth my effort. Some of my very best work has come from this wood kiln.

John Neely's (Logan, Utah) and Chuck Hindes' (Iowa City, Iowa) wood kilns and firing techniques give softer hues tending to blues and greys. I am fond of this palette and enjoy working with both artists, who are also friends, and I am always "pumped up" and ready for new things after working with them.

I might point out that my studio and home in Bissett, Manitoba is at

continued on page 71

4. **Carved Bottle**, 1996
stoneware; woodfired in
Utah State University's train
kiln, Logan
17 x 9" diameter

5. **Teapot**, 1997
stoneware; woodfired in
The University of Iowa's
anagama kiln, Iowa City; lid:
cast bronze (lost wax
method)
7 1/2 x 6 1/2 x 8"

6. **Carved Vase**, 1997
stoneware; woodfired in
Dan Anderson's "Mounds"
anagama kiln, Edwardsville,
Illinois
15 x 12 1/2" diameter

5.

6.

4.

John Balistreri

American, born 1962

"My recent work has been a continuation of my involvement with the ancient process of woodfiring. Since 1994, I began to concentrate on using the process of woodfiring to make objects that resonate with age, both geologic and human. I have built objects from our mechanized, industrial world that are recognizable to the viewer; such as barrels, anvils, wrenches, and jugs. The construction and firing of these objects transform them into contemporary artifacts, which ties geologic and human history to our contemporary condition.

In addition to industrial objects, I have been making pieces which are more universal in content, directly reflecting nature. The forms combine both biological and geological elements, which are also subjected to the violent, transforming process of the wood kiln.

Most recently I have begun to incorporate the figure into both veins of my work via heads and brains. This allows an expanded sense of narrative that implicates modern man's tenuous relationship to his environment both natural and artificial."

8.

7. ***Big Anvil #2***, 1998
   stoneware; woodfired in the
   artist's anagama kiln,
   Bowling Green, Ohio
   21 x 44 x 12"

8. ***Geoganic Form #10***, 1998
   stoneware with slips;
   woodfired in the artist's
   anagama kiln, Denver,
   Colorado
   15 x 29 x 21"

9. ***Geoganic Form #1***, 1997
   stoneware; woodfired in the
   artist's anagama kiln,
   Bowling Green, Ohio
   22 x 28 x 22"

9.

7.

Rob Barnard

American, born 1949

"When I first began making woodfired work, my teacher, Yagi Kazuo, warned me that if I couldn't use bland commercial clay and glazes and an electric kiln to make interesting pottery then I had no business fooling around with something as difficult and challenging as woodfiring. Of course, he wasn't talking about the technical side of woodfiring - the ability to fire a kiln and achieve certain dramatic effects. By difficult he meant the ability to discern real artistic achievement from the kind of accidental and random transformation that occurs when clay is subjected to the intense atmosphere and temperature of a woodfired kiln. He recognized the seductive nature of the process and the appeal of scorched clay and brilliant runny glaze and he cautioned me against letting that become the main force behind the work I made.

Woodfiring, Yagi felt, could become a crutch and hinder the growth and development of a potter by giving one the illusion of success when, in fact, that so-called success was entirely the result of the fortuitous interaction of natural elements like fire and clay. To him, art was not about the physical structure of a work but, rather, the artist's spiritual struggle that supports that structure.

This spiritual struggle by the artist to come to some kind of understanding of one's own absolutely inconsistent existence was to Yagi the "raison d'etre" for making art.

It seems to me that woodfiring only has meaning when it is used as a tool to challenge one's own preconceptions about the nature of beauty and, consequently, begins to make us think about what it means to be human. But if woodfiring is used as a refuge from the burden of artistic responsibility, like one of those machines found at county fairs across the country that spins a canvas while you drip different color

continued on page 71

10. *Tea Set*, 1998
  stoneware; woodfired
  teapot: 8 x 7 1/4 x 6 1/2"; 4
  cups: 4 x 2 1/3" diameter
  (each)

11. *Vase*, 1998
  stoneware; woodfired
  9 5/8 x 3 7/8" diameter

12. *Bowl*, 1998
  stoneware; woodfired
  3 3/8 x 7 1/2" diameter

11.

12.

10.

Joe Bruhin

American, born 1953

"Making pottery, for me, is a vehicle for spiritual growth. By opening myself, allowing spirit to enter, and by acting spontaneously, pots are born. The aim is to communicate with the eventual user, producing an aesthetic experience which I hope will improve the quality of his or her life.

Woodfiring is the best way for me to achieve these goals. As too much control removes the spirit, the element of chance here becomes a positive. By being in harmony with the elements and the forces of nature, the pot becomes a sacrificial offering. Surrendered to the flames and reborn, it aspires toward the ideals of timeless beauty and magic."

13. ***Temple Jar***, 1998
stoneware, red and white slip; woodfired in the artist's noborigama kiln
18 x 15" diameter

14. ***Jar***, 1998
stone embedded stoneware; woodfired on its side on seashells in the artist's noborigama kiln
9 3/4 x 10 3/4" diameter
Collection of Dr. and Mrs. Warren Boop, Little Rock, Arkansas

15. ***Bottle***, 1998
stone embedded porcelain; woodfired on its side on seashells in the artist's noborigama kiln
7 x 5" diameter
Collection of Denis Healy & Associates, Plano, Texas

14.

15.

13.

Peter Callas

American, born 1951

"History reflects the achievements of woodfiring over centuries of multiple use applications. Regarding the merits of anagama kilns - it is an elusive art form but as a tool for Modern art, this type of woodfire kiln has helped me to reach pinnacles of self-expression. Reflecting on the essence of an artist's statement, all I could think of was "how it changed my life." "It" being woodfiring and the underlying information one assimilates sublimely. Since 1992, my commitment to using the pyrometer to analyze ash behavior opened up whole new avenues of creative freedom. It elevated my firing technique to accommodate my aesthetic values in a "surgical strike type" of approach. After all, we are painting with fire, it is just simply a matter of form and color range."

16. ***Ghost***, 1994
stoneware; woodfired in an anagama kiln
32 1/2 x 19 x 18"

17. ***Child***, 1996
stoneware; woodfired in an anagama kiln
37 1/4 x 19 x 17 1/2"

16.

17.

Paul Chaleff

American, born 1947

"Our presence within this universe is precarious yet we have been able to find meaning and beauty within our small sphere of time and our limit of understanding.

I am concerned with chance, impurity, the fundamentals of earth, water and fire; the risk it takes to develop life from these elements and the skill it takes to create and define ideas from them. Many of my works are woodfired objects that refer to function. Their strength derives from their being rough, gestural, split, and impure. They talk of labor, history, of man's struggle to live in and endeavor to control nature.

My latest vessels are large glazed cogs, cones, cauldrons, and crucibles. This series explores the concept of labor beyond the capacity of the individual - group efforts. Each form represents a primitive ritualistic machine that refers to grinding, mixing, casting; yet is not a copy of anything which actually exists. I want each piece to exist seemingly without effort, as if it were always there. I have, therefore, eliminated any specific cultural or time-based references in this work by creating understated and minimal forms. The materials which best speak of group effort are related to the origins of the separation of labor. The smelting of metal and the cutting of stone are tasks that require such specialized skills. I have tried, therefore, to create works that seem to exist materially somewhere between stone and metal. The cog form is meant to infer a possible grindstone or gear; to be both, yet neither. Although it is thrown on a potter's wheel, it appears heavy and massive. I developed the cauldron as a ritualistic food-mixing vessel. At six

continued on page 71

18. ***Jar Form With Clay Stroke***, 1996-97
    stoneware; woodfired in an anagama kiln
    35 1/2 x 30" diameter
    Courtesy of Mendelson Gallery, Washington Depot, Connecticut

19. ***Jar Form With Parallel Strokes (94j)***, 1997
    stoneware; woodfired in an anagama kiln
    31 x 29" diameter
    The Arkansas Arts Center Foundation Collection: Purchased with a gift from The Vineyard-in-the-Park

20. ***Jar Form With Paddle Pattern***, 1995
    stoneware; woodfired in an anagama kiln
    31 x 29 1/2" diameter
    Courtesy of Mendelson Gallery, Washington Depot, Connecticut

18.

20.

19.

Mark Hewitt

American, born in England 1955

"When I look at old North Carolina pots, and when making my own, I do so with eyes that are not southern, eyes that instead reflect a sensibility learned during my childhood and deepened during my early experiences as a potter in England. From my father and grandfather I have inherited a deeply ingrained sense of the breadth and complexity of ceramic culture. However, the way I look at pots now, and the sense of quality I have developed about pots, stems from the time I spent working with Michael Cardew in Cornwall.

Every clay has a feel, a quality like the cut of different cloth. This quality can vary from the seductive satin of porcelain to the cozy flannel of earthenware. North Carolina's stoneware clays have the relaxed, purposeful and unassuming quality of denim overalls. They can be clean and elegant but are prone to being unkempt and scruffy, even a little wild. Old pots made with clays that the potters themselves have dug and simply refined are vibrant to the touch, warm to the eye, and possess an elaborate microaesthetic that rewards attentive inspection. Clay has meaning and value beyond its physical properties; clay is a clue."

21. **Tall Domed Jar**, 1998
    stoneware; woodfired in the
    artist's "Groundhog" style
    anagama kiln
    28 x 12" diameter
    The Arkansas Arts Center
    Foundation Collection:
    Gift of Juan Buono.

22. **Gallon Wall Vase**, 1998
    stoneware; woodfired in the
    artist's "Groundhog" style
    anagama kiln
    15 x 7 1/2 x 5"

23. **Gallon Jar**, 1998
    stoneware; woodfired in the
    artist's "Groundhog" style
    anagama kiln
    11 1/4 x 9" diameter

22.

23.

21.

Chuck Hindes

American, born 1942

"The Japanese aesthetic, with reference to the tea ceremony and its use of unglazed ware, has been my main inspiration. The issue of gesture, movement, or animation has been important to my work for years. The plastic and gestural qualities of clay should be emphasized, not dulled or subdued with an opaque or transparent skin. For my work, the movement of the form is heightened with the orchestration of natural color created by woodfiring.

I feel woodfiring has enhanced my work providing a palette of colors and surface textures that strengthen my forms visually, rather than cover them with a superficial skin. Woodfiring draws the inherent colors in the clay to the surface where they form patterns. The intense interaction of fire and clay permanently etches the color into the pot. The resulting patterns of color and textures create a lasting visual record of the woodfiring."

24.

24. *Teapot*, 1998
 stoneware; woodfired in an
 anagama kiln
 9 x 6"

25. *Teabowl*, 1998
 stoneware; woodfired in an
 anagama kiln
 4 1/2 x 4 1/2" diameter

26. *Cylinder*, 1998
 stoneware; woodfired in an
 anagama kiln
 12 x 5" diameter

25.

26.

Randy James Johnston

American, born 1950

"The clay becomes an intimate token of the artist and intimate memory of the fire. The fire is an essential way of marking the surface and transforming the object and giving it life. The whole notion of firing the piece is its moment of transformation. When one looks at woodfired objects, the ideal would be to feel that one is witnessing intimacy and a sense of immediacy and energy - life informed by emotion."

28.

27. *Long Boat Form*, 1998
stoneware, kaolin slip;
woodfired in the artist's
noborigama kiln
27 x 8 x 4 1/2"

28. *Stacking Box Form*, 1998
stoneware, kaolin slip;
woodfired in the artist's
noborigama kiln
7 3/4 x 9 1/2 x 4"
Collection of June and
Edmond Freeman, Little
Rock, Arkansas

29. *Vase Form*, 1998
stoneware, kaolin slip;
woodfired in the artist's
noborigama kiln
15 x 9 x 5"

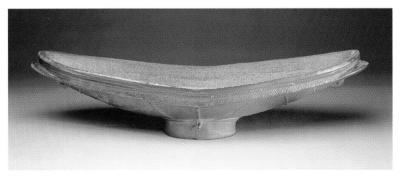

27.

29.

Karen Karnes

American, born 1925

30. ***Black Vessel (Tulip Vase)***, 1997
stoneware; woodfired
9 x 9 1/2 x 9"
Courtesy of materia/The Hand & The Spirit, Scottsdale, Arizona

31. ***Black & Green Vessel***, 1997
stoneware; woodfired
12 x 10 x 8"
Courtesy of materia/The Hand & The Spirit, Scottsdale, Arizona

32. ***Blue/Brown/Grey Vessel***, 1997
stoneware; woodfired
18 x 13 1/2 x 16"
The Arkansas Arts Center Foundation Collection: Purchased with a gift from The Vineyard-in-the-Park

30.

31.

32.

Maren Kloppmann

American, born in Germany 1962

"My work has been inspired by the concept of containment. The thrown pots I make seek their identity in the dialogue of form and function; the handbuilt coil vessels express, in their simplicity, the essence of the container.

The archetype of containment draws upon the human relationship with the ceramic vessel through time immemorial. Its qualitative nature is defined within the consistency of the containing substance - be it visible or not. A vessel may hold emotional space or memory, allowing the notion of volume to hold itself and fulfilling a function of contemplation through an imaginary substance. The vessel may hold water like a well: transparent liquid rendering the interior space and still giving sight to that which is filled. It may contain flour: the solid that nourishes creates in the vessel a new visible plane with its powdery consistency.

A vessel is defined by its linear properties, the plane of the walls and the volume, as well as the outer space it occupies. In the process of creating, it is my intent to work within these definitions regarding a minimal expression of form and surface. My goal is to give sculptural presence and functional purpose to vessel forms."

33. **Vessel**, 1998
    porcelain, terra sigillata and glaze; woodfired in a noborigama kiln
    10 x 13" diameter
    Collection of Peter Lippincott, Fort Smith, Arkansas

34. **Box**, 1998
    porcelain, terra sigillata and glaze; woodfired in a noborigama kiln
    4 x 7 x 3"
    Collection of Adrienne Taylor-Prissy, Little Rock, Arkansas

35. **Box**, 1998
    porcelain, terra sigillata and glaze; woodfired in a noborigama kiln
    3 1/2 x 5 x 3"
    Collection of Beverly Harlan, Little Rock, Arkansas

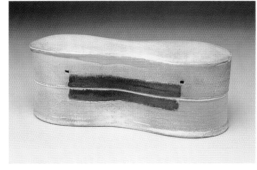

34.

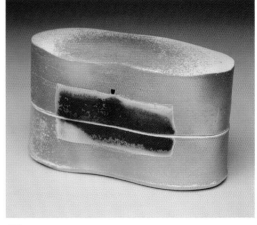

35.

33.

Peg Malloy

American, born 1943

"I want my pots to communicate the joy I feel while making them. In my work I strive for qualities of honesty, fluidity, and simplicity. In the process of making pots, I rely on intuition and feeling rather than intellectual argument and analysis. One pot leads to another and this evolution keeps me excited about clay.

I choose to fire with wood because I love the forms and surfaces highlighted by the warm colors and soft yellows of the wood ash deposits. I also welcome the element of surprise and the imperfections and irregularities that woodfiring brings to my work."

36.

36. *Altered Bowl*, 1998
porcelaneous stoneware; thrown and altered, woodfired in a bourry box style kiln
5 x 11 1/2 x 11"
Collection of Jean Mross, Bigelow, Arkansas

37. *Pitcher*, 1998
porcelaneous stoneware; thrown, woodfired in a bourry box style kiln
11 x 6 x 6"
Collection of David and Becky Dahlstedt, Mountain View, Arkansas

38. *Three Bottles*, 1998
porcelaneous stoneware; thrown and altered, woodfired in a bourry box style kiln
8 1/2 x 5 1/2 x 3 1/2";
7 3/4 x 5 1/2 x 3 1/2";
6 1/2 x 5 x 3"
Collection of Jim and Barbara Larkin, Hot Springs, Arkansas

38.

37.

Graham Marks

American, born 1951

39. **_Untitled_**, 1989
stoneware; coil construction,
woodfired in an anagama
kiln
34 1/2 x 32 1/2 x 34"
The Arkansas Arts Center
Foundation Collection:
Purchased with a gift from
The Vineyard-in-the-Park,
1991.
91.18

39.

Jan McKeachie-Johnston

American, born 1953

"I am a potter in rural Wisconsin. My work is functional, made either on a Leach style potter's wheel or with slabs of clay, or a combination of the two. I also enjoy using a pool cue to create forms from coils or cones of clay. A few of my strongest influences are African art, the pottery and art of the Minoan culture, American Indian art, and pots from the Japanese folk art tradition. I fire my work in a wood fueled noborigama kiln and a gas reduction kiln. I am excited by the inherent vitality which clay possesses as a material and about moving and marking it in a way that brings, I hope, a fresh and immediate feeling to it. Working with clay brings me much joy and fulfillment."

40. ***Tall Basket***, 1998
stoneware, kaolin slip;
woodfired in the artist's
noborigama kiln
18 1/2 x 6 x 6"

41. ***Small Ewer***, 1998
stoneware, kaolin slip;
woodfired in the artist's
noborigama kiln
9 x 7 x 5"
Collection of Dr. and Mrs.
Chester Hight, Little Rock,
Arkansas

42. ***Folded Slab Vase***, 1998
stoneware, kaolin slip;
woodfired in the artist's
noborigama kiln
6 x 6 x 4 1/2"
Collection of Jean Mross,
Bigelow, Arkansas

42.

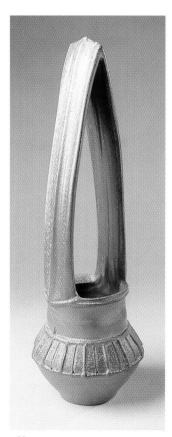

40.

41.

John Neely

American, born 1953

"Although most of what I make is intended for the dining table or kitchen, I am not dogmatic about utility. I think of utility as a kind of continuum, with the generic or universal idea of containment at one end, and specific, focused, single-purpose tools at the other. The teapot, a "machine" for brewing and serving tea, would be found at the specific end, but it also serves as a vehicle for my explorations into the materials and processes of ceramics. My approach lies somewhere between that of the alchemist and that of the scientist. Discovery, rather than expression, is my primary motivation."

43. *Teapot*, 1998
Stoneware; woodfired
6 1/2 x 8 1/2 x 5"

44. *Teapot (Grey)*, 1998
stoneware; woodfired
4 1/2 x 7 1/2 x 7"

44.

43.

Hiroshi Ogawa

American, born 1941

""Shibui" is a simple adjective which describes a profound, unassuming, quiet feeling. There is no exact English counterpart for this adjective. Nearest to it, perhaps, are words like austere, subdued and restrained. But to the Japanese, the word is more complex, suggesting quietness, depth, simplicity and purity. The beauty it describes is introversive; the beauty of inner illumination.

Pottery is not a project for the intellect; it is a project of the soul. The pots created speak of a beauty within. It is this beauty with inner implications that is referred to as "shibui". It is not a beauty displayed before the viewer by its creator but, rather, the beauty that the viewer himself draws out of that piece.

The idea of following in the footsteps of a tradition is a difficult one to fully understand from the perspective of western art which demands creative, novel ideas. The viewer must transcend the cultural differences in order to understand and appreciate these pots.

I hope the earth, water and fire that created these pots and their surface texture will stir your imagination to see the spirit within."

45. ***Vase #1025***, 1998
stoneware; woodfired in the artist's anagama/noborigama kiln
16 x 12" diameter

46. ***Magic Kiss***, 1998
stoneware; woodfired in the artist's anagama/noborigama kiln
16 x 12" diameter

47. ***Vase #1021***, 1998
stoneware; woodfired in the artist's anagama/noborigama kiln
16 x 12" diameter

45.

46.

47.

Don Reitz

American, born 1929

48.

48. *Tea Stack Pot*, 1998
stoneware; woodfired in
Dan Anderson's "Mounds"
anagama kiln, Edwardsville,
Illinois
27 1/2 x 11 1/2" diameter

49. *Jar*, 1994
stoneware; woodfired in
Frank Boyden's anagama
kiln, Otis, Oregon
19 x 14" diameter

50. *Footed Form*, 1995
stoneware; woodfired in
Peter Callas's anagama kiln,
Belvidere, New Jersey
8 x 18 x 13"

50.

49.

Mary Roehm

American, born 1951

51. _Untitled Large Bowl #1_,
1997
Porcelain; woodfired,
natural ash glaze
8 x 25 1/2" diameter
Courtesy of The Sybaris
Gallery, Royal Oak,
Michigan

52. _Untitled Medium Bowl_,
1997
porcelain; woodfired,
natural ash glaze
5 1/2 x 14" diameter
The Arkansas Arts Center
Foundation Collection:
Purchased with an
anonymous gift

53. _Two Small Tea Bowls_,
1997
porcelain; woodfired,
natural ash glaze
2 1/2 x 5" diameter;
3 x 5" diameter
Courtesy of The Sybaris
Gallery, Royal Oak,
Michigan

51.

53.

52.

Will Ruggles and Douglass Rankin

American, born 1956 and 1948, respectively

"Wood has always been our chosen method of firing. The kiln is our final tool - consummating by fire the effects of all previous efforts and revealing the true structure and feeling of the pot. No part of the forming and glazing process can hide behind the rigors of shrinkage and fluxing. The final arbitrator of beauty, the kiln takes pots of equal quality and makes one magnificent and another just all right or even ugly. It is as important to the effect of the finished pot as our hands, adding unforeseeable possibilities and potentials for beauty.

Another affection that we have for woodfiring is that the act of firing maintains intimacy with the pots through their completion. From how the pot is stacked, to the way we read and adjust the smoke, flame, temperature and heat rise, a firing personality develops. Throughout the loading and firing we make countless in-the-moment decisions and later respond to the results of those choices. Each in itself influences the look and feel of the pots. But also these choices impact and give history and character to all of the other decisions.

Our kiln and our firing style definitely impart a particular quality on the pots, and we fire each time with the same basic attitude and objectives. However, the nature of the kiln and of our relationship with it never allows for the same firing qualities from firing to firing or even between chambers. This capacity for the kiln, wood and firing method to take the final outcome of the pots out of our control is an extremely valuable tool for our aesthetic growth. Each load gives us new, exciting pots that spur us on to refinements in clay, glaze and slip making, decorating, kiln stacking, fuel choices, stoking method, salt and soda quantities, and final temperatures. In this way the cycle of making and firing continuously renews itself."

54.

54. *Rimmed Serving Bowl*,
1998
stoneware; woodfired in the
artist's noborigama kiln
3 1/2 x 11 3/8" diameter
Collection of Cindy Truax,
Little Rock, Arkansas

55. *Teapot*, 1998
stoneware; woodfired in the
artist's noborigama kiln
7 3/4 x 9 1/2 x 6 1/2"
Collection of James Evans,
Little Rock, Arkansas

56. *Square Vase*, 1998
stoneware; woodfired in the
artist's noborigama kiln
11 7/8 x 5 1/4" square
Collection of Jim and
Barbara Larkin, Hot Springs,
Arkansas

55.

56.

Jeff Shapiro

American, born 1949

"As a ceramic artist trained in Japan but living in the United States, I often ask myself "What direction should I be taking." I find myself in a unique position. Though I have a strong feeling and response to the woodfired work of Bizen and Shigaraki, I am neither Japanese nor working in Japan. My work has evolved using my Japanese experiences, an indelible love and reverence for clay, and the results of unglazed woodfiring techniques. I am also strongly influenced by the Japanese aesthetic or sensibility, particularly as it relates to nature.

I am striving to produce work that is enhanced by the woodfiring, but not determined by it. The clay, forms, loading, and firing are all integral parts of the finished piece. I believe strongly that the firing results are directly related to the clay and that those results need to be congruous with the forming technique. If not, the parts compete with each other and the presence of the piece will be diminished.

I draw from organic formations in nature such as stones. The stones may manifest themselves as stone impressions in clay surface or actual stones in the make up of the clay body; or as a cast form of a stone that is then worked to produce something from the original object."

57. ***Tea Bowl With Drips***,
1998
stoneware; unglazed,
woodfired in the artist's
anagama kiln
3 1/2 x 5 1/2" diameter

58. ***Vessel With Feet And
Handles***, 1998
stoneware; unglazed,
woodfired in the artist's
anagama kiln
7 1/2 x 10 1/4 x 9 5/8"
The Arkansas Arts Center
Foundation Collection

59. ***Stone Formation Vessel
#II***, 1998
stoneware; unglazed,
woodfired in the artist's
anagama kiln
12 x 12 x 8 1/2"

57.

59.

58.

Mark Shapiro

American, born 1955

"The pots I most admire - whether they be great Asian stoneware from the Song China, Yi Korean pots, Japanese folk pottery, early American saltware, old jugs from la Borne, France or the pots of Leach, Hamada and their followers - were made in great quantities by potters who worked everyday and fired large woodburning kilns. I follow this practice, not as formula for making good pots, but because it is the best way I can see to make contemporary pots which have power, presence and purpose."

60. *Jar With Unglazed Bands,*
1998
stoneware, glaze; woodfired in the artist's nobrigama kiln
12 1/2 x 11 1/4" diameter

61. *Stepped Covered Jar With Amber Glaze*, 1998
stoneware, glaze; woodfired in the artist's nobrigama kiln
4 3/4 x 10 1/4 x 6"
Collection of Dan and Caroline Anderson, Edwardsville, Illinois

62. *Faceted Box With Black Slip On Slip Decoration*,
1998
stoneware, slip; woodfired in the artist's nobrigama kiln
7 1/2 x 5 3/4" diameter
Collection of Denis Healy & Associates, Plano, Texas

62.

61.

60.

Jane Shellenbarger

American, born 1964

"My ceramic work focuses on the vessel aesthetic, primarily on altered and decorated forms. While function continues to be a primary concern, I am equally interested in decoration and embellishment of surface. I work in both porcelain and stoneware clays, firing with soda and wood; often the pieces undergo multi-firing or are enameled and sandblasted to achieve a depth of surface. Many of the pieces are fired in a wood burning anagama style kiln and are fired continuously for up to four days. I am interested in the dialogue that clay creates with hand and eye memory."

63.

63. *Teapot*, 1998
stoneware; woodfired in the
artist's anagama kiln
9 x 7 x 5"

64. *Oil Can Ewer*, 1998
stoneware, enamel;
woodfired in the artist's
anagama kiln
9 x 5 x 4"

65. *Triangular Box*, 1998
stoneware, enamel;
woodfired in the artist's
anagama kiln
6 x 5 x 5"

65.

64.

John Skelton

American, born 1974

"My work as an artist is devoted to functional pottery. My work has its innate origins in utility although I do have interests in some pots being more objects of beauty or aesthetics. The functional aspect of pottery is unique to art mediums in that each pot has an underlying purpose. This purpose is important to me. Seeing the final piece in use is a primary source of inspiration. Beginning with a vessel in mind, an idea is formed for how it will function in relation to human touch. The feeling of a strongly balanced handle or the smooth flow of a pouring spout are examples of what I find essential to functional pots. Likewise, the weight should be comfortable and make sense with the form.

The tactile feeling of a pot is also important in its visual feeling. My work is very much about myself, not just on an academic level but on an intuitive level. In some ways my art is confessional because I allow myself to come out in my work. I want to use the tools of intuition to create pots. I think this allows deeper parts of myself to come out in the work. I like how people can look at my work and see me. My pots are in depth but quiet and simple. Soft, warm earth tones and brushwork patterns create layers of visual depth on strong simplified forms. The decorated surfaces are treated in two ways. They are treated as reflections of the forms in order to emphasize the feeling of a piece or as complements to the forms in order to create a unified balance in a piece. Stenciled images of birds fly around the pots often hidden under brushed patterns as though the birds are an image woven on fabric. Birds are also revealed on surfaces through large streaky brushstrokes of rainy grays. It is my intention to allow myself to come out in the work through intuition more than through personal analysis. Ideas and metaphors come to the surface through these layered decorations but the pots as a whole are expressions of myself more by their feeling."

66. **Stacked Ewer**, 1998
    stoneware; wood/salt fired
    6 x 8 3/4 x 5"
    Collection of Marie E. Dow,
    Little Rock, Arkansas

67. **Black & White Vase**, 1998
    stoneware; wood/salt fired
    11 3/4 x 5 1/2 x 3 1/2"

68. **Stacked Box**, 1998
    stoneware; wood/salt fired
    8 1/2 x 5 x 5"

66.

68.

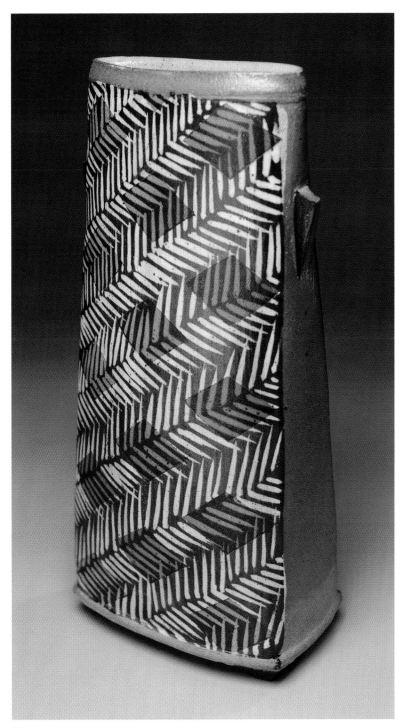

67.

Byron Temple

American, born 1933

"I have confined myself to creating art - a subtle fusion of aristocratic and popular culture. Pots, like children, have to make their own path in the world, eventually."

69. **Loop Button Jar (BT No. 1)**, 1998
porcelain, seashells, salt; woodfired in an anagama kiln
5 1/2 x 5" diameter

70. **Button Jar (BT No. 2)**, 1998
porcelain; woodfired in an anagama kiln
4 1/4 x 6" diameter
Collection of Gayle Batson, Little Rock, Arkansas

71. **Knob Button Jar (BT No. 3)**, 1998
porcelain; woodfired in an anagama kiln
4 3/8 x 6 1/8" diameter

69.

70.

71.

Skeff Thomas

American, born 1964

"My work is fired in a "fast-fire" wood kiln constructed of insulating fire brick. The firings range from 9 to 14 hours using pine as a fuel source. Because this type of woodfiring is comparatively short to kilns of other designs and construction, I agitate the ashes in the fire box during the lower temperatures to induce a larger deposit of fly ash on the ware. The kiln is filled with the ware of only two or three potters who are doing the firing. This provides (demands) a personal connection with the kiln during each firing. Generally the potters who are doing the firing collect the wood and are with the kiln for the whole firing. Small amounts of salt and baking soda are introduced into the kiln after 2200°F, providing the ware with a slight gloss.

The woodfiring process provides an intimate connection between myself and the final transformation of the pottery. The kiln is an integral part of the final outcome, and understanding the needs of the kiln during the firing enable the potter to achieve the desired temperature and finished results. I respond to the immediacy of the firing, and the simple complexity which is inherent in the process. Because the kiln does play an integral part in the transformation process, I apply a minimal decoration or glaze to the exterior surface of the ware. I am interested in working with different color clay bodies that have a fine coating of slip applied to the surface. The different slips provide a range of colors depending on the firing, location in the kiln, and amount of sodium introduced into the kiln. What is important is that the strength of the form is complemented by the firing."

72. _Pitcher_, 1998
porcelain, slip decoration; woodfired in the artist's Olsen fast-fire kiln
18 x 9 x 7"
Collection of Denis Healy & Associates, Plano, Texas

73. _Vase_, 1998
stoneware, slip decoration; woodfired in the artist's Olsen fast-fire kiln
21 x 9 x 9"
Collection of Georges Launet, Little Rock, Arkansas

74. _Casserole_, 1998
stoneware, slip decoration; woodfired in the artist's Olsen fast-fire kiln
8 x 11 x 11"
Collection of David and Becky Dahlstedt, Mountain View, Arkansas

72.

74.

73.

Jack Troy

American, born 1938

"I use no glazes or slips of any kind, preferring to rely on the inconsistencies of the firing process to add texture and color to the work. Knowing that I will never be able to preordain the exact outcome of the firings enables me to concentrate on those aspects of the process I can control, such as selection of the clays, placement of the pieces in specific "zones" of the kiln, and maintaining the four-day firing to as high a standard as I can manage.

If serendipitous events enliven my work, they result from my devotion to both care and prayer."

75. *Traditional Jug*, 1998
   stoneware, natural ash glaze; woodfired in the artist's anagama kiln
   10 1/2 x 8" diameter

76. *Vase*, 1997
   porcelain, natural ash glaze; woodfired in the artist's anagama kiln
   9 x 4 3/4" diameter

77. *Paddled Pot*, 1998
   porcelain, natural ash glaze; woodfired in the artist's anagama kiln
   12 x 9 1/2 x 9 1/2"

77.

75.

76.

Biographies

Dan Anderson

Old Poag Road Clay and Glass
5519 Old Poag Road
Edwardsville, Illinois 62025-7417

Studio potter
Professor, Head of Ceramics, Department of Art
    and Design, Southern Illinois University at
    Edwardsville

Education:
1968   B.S., Art Education, University of
            Wisconsin-River Falls
1970   M.F.A., Ceramics, Cranbrook Academy of
            Art, Bloomfield Hills, MI

Travel:
Italy, Europe, South Africa, South Korea, Australia

Selected Exhibitions:
1993   *The Tea Party*, American Craft Museum,
            New York, NY
        NCECA 1993 Clay National, San Diego
            Museum of Art, CA
        The 29th Ceramic National, Everson
            Museum, Syracuse, NY
        *Earth, Air, Fire and Water: Elements of the
            Permanent Collection*, Cranbrook
            Museum of Art, Bloomfield Hills, MI
1994   *Ceramic and Fiber: A New Generation*,
            Charles A. Wustum Museum of Fine
            Arts, Racine, WI
        *Building the Cranbrook Collection:
            Acquisitions during Roy Slade's Tenure
            (1977-1994)*, Cranbrook Museum of
            Art, Bloomfield Hills, MI
1996   *52nd Scripps Ceramic Annual Exhibition*,
            Scripps College, Claremont, CA
1997   *Urban Interpretations*, Coburn Art Gallery,
            The Colorado College, Colorado Springs
        Wood-Fire Invitational, George Caleb
            Bingham Gallery, Missouri University,
            Columbia
1998   *Pittsburgh Collects Clay*, Carnegie Museum
            of Art, Pittsburgh, PA

Selected Public Collections:
Archie Bray Foundation for the Ceramic Arts,
    Helena, MT
The Arkansas Arts Center, Little Rock
Boise Art Museum, ID
Carnegie Museum of Art, Pittsburgh, PA
Cranbrook Art Museum, Bloomfield Hills, MI
Everson Museum of Art, Syracuse, NY
Ewha Women's University, Seoul, Korea
Philadelphia Museum of Art, PA
Frederick R. Weisman Art Museum,
    Minneapolis, MN
Charles A. Wustum Museum of Fine Arts,
    Racine, WI

Robert Archambeau

52 175 Allegheny Drive
Winnipeg, Manitoba R3T3A1
Canada

Studio potter

Education:
1959   B.F.A., Studio Arts, Bowling Green
            University, OH
1964   M.F.A., Studio Ceramics, New York State
            College of Ceramics at Alfred University

Travel:
France, Italy, Greece, Turkey, Cypress, Sardinia,
Crete, Algeria, Puerto Rico, Mexico, China,
Japan, South Korea

Selected Public Collections:
Archie Bray Foundation for the Ceramic Arts,
    Helena, MT
The Canada Council Art Bank
Canadian Glass and Clay Museum,
    Waterloo, Ontario
Glenbow-Alberta Institute, Calgary,
    Alberta, Canada
Southern Illinois University at Edwardsville
The International Museum of Ceramic Art,
    New York State College of Ceramics at Alfred
The Toledo Museum of Art, OH
The Winnipeg Art Gallery, Winnipeg,
    Manitoba, Canada

John Balistreri

1946 East 66 Avenue
Denver, Colorado 80229
or
204 Haskins Road
Bowling Green, Ohio 43402

Ceramic artist
Assistant Professor of Ceramics, Bowling Green
    State University, OH

Education:
1986   B.F.A., Kansas City Art Institute, MO
1988   M.F.A., Kent State University, OH

Selected Exhibitions:
1990   *46th Scripps Ceramic Annual*, Scripps
            College, Claremont, CA
1992   Solo Exhibition, Wichita Center for the Arts,
            KS
1993   *Colorado Clay*, Foothills Center for the Arts,
            Denver, CO
1994   *Fire Men: Masters of the Anagama Kiln*,
            Leedy Voulkos Gallery, Kansas City, MO
1995   *Keepers of the Flame: Students of Ken
            Ferguson*, Kemper Museum
            Contemporary Art and Design,
            Kansas City, MO
        NCECA Clay National, Frederick R.
            Weisman Art Museum, Minneapolis, MN

Selected Public Collections:
Adams County Historical Society, Denver, CO
State Fair Community College, Slauda, MO
Kent State University, OH
Kansas City Art Institute, Kansas City, MO
University of Oregon, Eugene

Rob Barnard

597 South Middle Road
Timberville, Virginia 22853

Studio potter

Education:
1971 Studied pottery, University of Kentucky,
        Lexington
1974 Research student under Kazuo Yagi,
        Kyoto University of Fine Arts, Japan

Travel:
Japan 1974-1978, 1984, 1989, 1992, 1995

Selected Exhibitions:
1986 *Spotlight '86*, University of Florida,
        Gainesville
1988 Rasdall Gallery, University of Kentucky,
        Lexington
1989 *Fragile Blossom, Enduring Earth: The
        Japanese Influence on American Ceramics*,
        Everson Museum, Syracuse, NY
1992 Meitetsu Department Store, Nagoya, Japan
        *Ceramic Dialogues, Shiro Otani & Rob
        Barnard*, Japan Information and
        Cultural Center, Japan Embassy,
        Washington, DC
        Revolving Techniques, James A. Michener
        Art Museum, Doylestown, PA
1995 *Beyond East and West: A Rob Barnard
        Retrospective 1974-1994*, Sasakawa
        Peace Foundation, Washington, DC
1996 Japan American Society, Washington, DC
        Virginia Clay, Longwood Center for the
        Visual Arts, Farmville, VA
1998 Longwood Center for the Visual Arts,
        Farmville, VA

Selected Public Collections:
American Craft Museum, New York, NY
Everson Museum of Art, Syracuse, NY
Dickinson College, Carlisle, PA
Japan Embassy, Washington, DC
Millersville University, PA
Renwick Gallery of the National Museum
  of American Art, Smithsonian Institution,
  Washington, DC

Joe Bruhin

Route 64 West, Box 247-B
Fox, Arkansas 72051

Studio potter

Education:
1979-80 Meremac Community College,
           Kirkwood, MO
1981   Maryville College, St. Louis, MO
1982-83 Artist in Residence, Idaho State
           University, Sun Valley Center
           for the Arts

Travel:
Europe, North Africa, Asia

Selected Exhibitions:
1983 *Vessels Aesthetic*, Taft College Art Gallery,
        CA
1992 *Regional Craft Biennial*, The Arkansas
        Arts Center, Little Rock
1993 *Arkansas: Year of American Craft 1993*,
        The Arkansas Arts Center, Little Rock
1995 *Super Bowls*, Arizona State University Art
        Museum, Tucson
1997 *Art in America: Inaugural Exhibit*,
        The Washington Design Center, DC

Selected Public Collections:
The Arkansas Arts Center, Little Rock
Arkansas Arts Council, Little Rock
Lyons College, Batesville, AR
The Peoria Art Guild, Peoria, IL
Saint Louis Community College, St. Louis, MO

Peter Callas

One Orchard Street
Belvidere, New Jersey 07823

Studio potter/sculptor

Education:
1973   B.F.A., University of Ouget Sound,
           Tacoma, WA
1973-74 Artist in Residence, Archie Bray
           Foundation, Helena, MT

Travel:
Japan, Norway, Sweden, Netherlands, Australia

Selected Exhibitions:
1991 University of Oregon Art Museum, Eugene
        Tacoma Art Museum, WA
        Cheney-Cowles Memorial Museum,
          Spokane, WA
        Morris Museum, Morris Township, NJ
1992 Erie Art Museum, PA
        Nora Eccles Harrison Museum of Art,
          Logan, UT
        The Cleveland Museum of Art, OH
1993 The Kunstindustrimuseet Museum,
          Oslo, Norway
        The Museum of Fine Arts, Lillehammer,
          Norway
1997 The Shigaraki Ceramic Cultural Park
          Museum, Japan

Selected Public Collections:
Archie Bray Foundation for the Ceramic Arts,
  Helena, MT
The Art Space, Seoul, Korea
The Cleveland Museum of Art, OH
Florida Keys Community College, Key West
Gotoh Art Museum, Tokyo, Japan
Philadelphia Museum of Art, PA
The Shigaraki Ceramic Cultural Park, Japan
University of Central Florida, Orlando
University of Iowa Museum of Art, Iowa City

Paul Chaleff

P.O. Box 648
Pine Plains, New York 12567

Studio potter

Education:
1969   B.A., City College of New York, NY
1971   M.F.A., City University of New York, NY
1976   Nakazato Studio, Karatsu, Japan
1977, 1981 Morioka Studio, Wakayama, Japan

Travel:
Japan

Selected Exhibitions:
1982 *Fires and Ashes*, Pittsburgh Center
        for the Arts, PA
1985 *Clay Everyday Plus Sunday*,
        Kohler Arts Center, Sheboygan, WI
1986 *Clay in the East*, Maryland Institute,
        Baltimore

1987 *Japanese Influences*, Japan Society,
       New York, NY
1988 *Design*, Museum of Modern Art,
       New York, NY
1989 *Fragile Blossom, Enduring Earth: The
       Japanese Influence on American
       Ceramics*, Everson Museum of Art,
       Syracuse, NY
1990 *Ashen Beauty*, University of Oregon
       Museum of Art, Eugene
1991 *American Woodfire '91*, University of Iowa
       Museum of Art, Iowa City
1994 *Joan Mannheimer Collects*, University of
       Iowa Museum of Art, Iowa City
1998 *Clay and Friendship-Contemporary
       Ceramics: Korean and American
       Connections*, Korean Cultural Center
       Gallery, New York, NY

Selected Public Collections:
American Craft Museum, New York, NY
The Arkansas Arts Center, Little Rock
The Brooklyn Museum, NY
Carnegie Institute, Pittsburgh, PA
Everson Museum of Art, Syracuse, NY
Los Angeles County Museum of Art, CA
The Metropolitan Museum of Art, New York, NY
Museum of Modern Art, New York, NY
Museum of Fine Arts, Boston, MA
Renwick Gallery of the National Museum of
    American Art, Smithsonian Institution,
    Washington, DC

Mark Hewitt

W. M. Hewitt Pottery
424 Johnny Burke Road
Pittsboro, North Carolina 27312

Studio potter

Education:
1976-79 Apprenticed with Michael Cardew,
        Wenford Bridge Pottery, Bodmin,
        England
1979-82 Apprenticed with Todd Picker, Cornwall
        Bridge Pottery, Cornwall Bridge, CT

Travel:
West Africa, Taiwan, Japan, Korea

Selected Exhibitions:
1992 *Stuck in Mud*, Western Carolina University,

Cullowhee, NC
1993 *Wholly Land: Pots from North Carolina*,
       Harlequin Gallery, London, England
1997 *Mark Hewitt: Potter*, North Carolina State
       University, Raleigh

Selected Public Collections:
The Ackland Museum, University of North
    Carolina, Chapel Hill
The Arkansas Arts Center, Little Rock
Chrysler Museum, Norfolk, VA
City of Stoke-on-Trent Museum, Staffordshire,
    England
Executive Mansion, Raleigh, NC
Mint Museum of Art, Charlotte, NC
National Arboretum, Washington, DC
National Carolina Arboretum, Raleigh, NC

Chuck Hindes

728 East Fairchild Street
Iowa City, Iowa 52245

Studio potter
Professor of Ceramics, School of Art, University
    of Iowa

Education:
1966 B.F.A., University of Illinois at Urbana-
       Champaign
1968 M.F.A., Rhode Island School of Design,
       Providence

Selected Exhibitions:
1990 *Ashen Beauty*, Tacoma Art Museum, WA
1992 *Woodfire Ceramics*, Gallery of Art, Boise
       State University, ID
1993 *Invitational Ceramics and Drawing
       Exhibition*, University of Wisconsin-
       Whitewater
       Contrasts in Clay: Two Iowa Potters,
       MacNider Museum, Mason City, IA
       *The Legacy of the Archie Bray Foundation:
       A Celebration of Ceramic Art 1951-
       1992*, Bellevue Art Museum, WA
1995 *Feats of Clay*, Lincoln Art Center, CA
       Ceramics U.S.A., Center for the Visual
       Arts, University of North Texas, Denton
1997 *Woodfire Invitational*, Wright Museum
       of Art, Beloit College, WI
       Woodfire Invitational, College of the
       Ozarks, Lookout Point, MO

1998 *28th Annual Invitational Ceramics
       Exhibition: Woodfire*, Crossman Gallery,
       University of Wisconsin-Whitewater

Selected Public Collections:
Archie Bray Foundation for the Ceramic Arts,
    Helena, MT
Brigham Young University, Provo, UT
Everson Museum of Art, Syracuse, NY
The International Museum of Ceramic Art,
    New York State College of Ceramics at Alfred
Sioux City Art Center, IA
The Saint Louis Art Museum, MO

Randy James Johnston

N 8336 690th Street
River Falls, Wisconsin 54022

Studio potter
Associate Professor of Ceramics, University of
    Wisconsin-River Falls

Education:
1972 B.F.A., Studio Arts, University of Minnesota,
       MN
1975 Studied with Shimaoka Tatsuzo, Mashiko,
       Japan
1990 M.F.A., Ceramics, Southern Illinois
       University at Edwardsville

Travel:
Japan

Selected Exhibitions:
1990 *Fragile Blossom, Enduring Earth: The
       Japanese Influence on American
       Ceramics*, American Craft Museum,
       New York, NY
1992 *Studio Potter Twentieth Anniversary
       Collection*, Manchester Institute of
       Arts & Sciences, NH
       NCECA Clay National, University of
       Arizona, Tempe
1994 *Warren MacKenzie Sphere of Influence
       Invitational*, Southern Illinois University
       at Edwardsville
1995 *NCECA Clay National*, Frederick R.
       Weisman Art Museum, Minneapolis, MN
       Invitational, University of North Carolina,
       Charlotte
1996 *First Mashiko International Ceramics*, Japan

1997 *Shimaoka, MacKenzie, Matsuzaki, Johnston*, Ikebukuro Seibu Gallery, Tokyo, Japan
  Woodfire Invitational, College of the Ozarks, Point Lookout, MO
1998 Invitational, Boston Society of Arts and Crafts, MA

Selected Public Collections:
Emison Art Center, Greencastle, IN
Hamada Shoji Foundation, Japan
Government of Norway
Minnesota Historical Society, St. Paul
University Art Museum, University of Arizona, Tempe
University Art Museum, University of Minnesota, Minneapolis
Frederick R. Weisman Art Museum, Minneapolis, MN

Karen Karnes

HC 70 Box 64A
Star Route
Morgan, Vermont 05853

Studio potter

Education:
1946 Brooklyn College, New York
1951-52 New York State College of Ceramics at Alfred University

Selected Exhibitions:
1964 *Objects U.S.A.*, Smithsonian Institution, Washington, DC
1968 *American Studio Pottery*, Victoria & Albert Museum, London, England
1972 *International Ceramics*, Victoria & Albert Museum, London, England
1976 *Soup Tureens*, Campbell Museum, Camden, NJ
1978 *Craft Art and Religion*, Vatican Museum, Rome, Italy
1979 *Century of Ceramics in the U.S.*, Everson Museum of Art, Syracuse, NY
1982 *Pots and Potters*, Aldeburgh, England
1985 *High Styles: American Design Since 1900*, Whitney Museum of American Art, New York, NY

Selected Public Collections:
American Craft Museum, New York, NY
The Arkansas Arts Center, Little Rock
Cranbrook Museum of Art, Bloomfield Hills, MI
Delaware Museum of Art, Wilmington
The Detroit Institute of Arts, MI
Everson Museum of Art, Syracuse, NY
Los Angeles County Museum of Art, CA
Philadelphia Museum of Art, PA
The Metropolitan Museum of Art, New York, NY
Ruckland Museum, New Zealand
The Saint Louis Art Museum, MO
Victoria & Albert Museum, London, England

Maren Kloppmann

106 N. Sherburne Street
Stillwater, Minnesota 55082

Studio potter
Exhibition Coordinator, Northern Clay Center, Minneapolis, MN

Education:
1984 Diploma as Journeyman, Keramik Handwerkskammer, Germany
1993 B.F.A., Ceramics, Kansas City Art Institute, MO
1996 M.F.A., Ceramics, University of Minnesota, Minneapolis

Selected Exhibitions:
1994 *Minnesota Clay*, Rochester Art Center, MN
1996 *26th Annual Ceramics Exhibition*, University of Wisconsin-Whitewater
  Thesis Exhibition, Katherine E. Nash Gallery, Minneapolis, MN
  Women in Clay, Rochester Art Center, MN
1997 *Vessel and Sculpture*, Winona State University, MN
1998 *For the House and Garden*, Pewabic Pottery, Detroit, MI

Selected Public Collections:
The Arkansas Arts Center, Little Rock
Frederick R. Weisman Art Museum, Minneapolis, MN
Historical Society of Minnesota, Minneapolis

Peg Malloy

210 Stark Mesa Road
Carbondale, Colorado 81623

Studio potter
Instructor, Carbondale Clay Center, CO

Education:
  Brooks Institute of Photography, Santa Barbara, CA
1966-67 Apprenticed with Henry Mead
1983 Jeff Oestreich, Summer Vale Workshop, CO
1988 David Shaner, Anderson Ranch Arts Center, Snowmass Village, CO
1989 Chris Staley, Anderson Ranch Arts Center, Snowmass Village, CO
  Ken Ferguson, Summer School, University of Colorado, Boulder
1991 Ken Price, Anderson Ranch Arts Center, Snowmass, CO
1994 Sandy Simon, Anderson Ranch Arts Center, Snowmass, CO

Selected Exhibitions:
1990 *American Woodfire '91*, The University of Iowa, Iowa City
1992 *Utilitarian Clay: Celebrate the Object*, Arrowmont School of Arts and Crafts, Gatlinburg, TN
  Colorado Clay, The Foothills Art Center, Golden, CO
  The Clay Cup IV, Southern Illinois University, Carbondale
1994 *The Teapot Show*, University of Northern Colorado, Greeley
  The 1994 International Orton Cone Box Show, Baker University, Baldwin, KS
1996 *Western Clay: A 3D Feature*, University of Southern Colorado, Pueblo
  The 1996 International Orton Cone Box Show, Baker University, Baldwin City, KS
1997 *Wood Fired Ceramics*, University of the Ozarks, Point Lookout, MO
1998 *Women Who Fire with Wood*, Andrews University, Berrien Springs, MI

Graham Marks

4635 East Valley Road
Andover, New York 14806

Former studio potter
Former Head of Ceramics, Cranbrook Academy
    of Art, Bloomfield Hills, MI
Acupuncturist
Education:
1974   B.F.A., Philadelphia College of Art, PA
1976   M.F.A., New York State College of
            Ceramics, Division of Art and Design,
            Alfred University

Selected Exhibitions:
1985   *Contemporary American Ceramics: Twenty
            Artists*, Newport Harbor Art Museum,
            CA
1986   Everson Museum of Art, Syracuse, NY
            Contemporary Arts: An Expanding View,
            Wellesley College Museum, MA
1986   *Craft Today: Poetry of the Physical*,
            American Craft Museum, New York, NY
1987   *The Eloquent Object*, The Philbrook
            Museum of Art, Tulsa, OK
1988   *Power Over the Clay: American Studio
            Potters*, Detroit Institute of Arts, MI
1989   *Surface and Form, A Union of Polarities in
            Contemporary Ceramics*, The National
            Museum of Ceramic Art, Baltimore, MD
            Craft Today U.S.A., Musée des Arts
            Décoratifs, Paris, France
1990   *Building a Permanent Collection:
            Perspectives on the 1980s*, American
            Craft Museum, New York, NY
            *Clay, Color, Content: 28th Ceramic
            National*, Everson Museum of Art,
            Syracuse, NY

Selected Public Collections:
American Craft Museum, New York, NY
The Arkansas Arts Center, Little Rock
Cranbrook Academy of Art Museum,
    Bloomfield Hills, MI
Everson Museum of Art, Syracuse, NY
Memorial Art Gallery of the University of
    Rochester, NY
The International Museum of Ceramic Art,
    New York State College of Ceramics at Alfred
Rochester Institute of Technology, NY
University of Colorado, Boulder
University of Iowa Museum of Art, Iowa City

Jan McKeachie-Johnston

N 8336 690th Street
River Falls, Wisconsin 54022

Studio artist

Education:
1976   Quadna Summer Art Center
1978   University of Minnesota, Minneapolis
1990   Southern Illinois University at Edwardsville

Travel:
Chile

Selected Exhibitions:
1988   *Midwest Clay Invitational*, University of
            Northern Iowa, Cedar Falls
1990   *Juried Undergraduate Show*, Southern
            Illinois University at Edwardsville
1991   *Juried National*, San Angelo Museum of
            Fine Arts, TX
1993   *Warren MacKenzie and Friends*, Bluffton
            College, OH
1994   *Warren MacKenzie Sphere of Influence
            Invitational*, Southern Illinois University
            at Edwardsville
1995   *Across the Big Muddy*, Phipps Center for the
            Arts, Hudson, WI
            Women in Clay, Rochester Art Center, MN
            Ceramics Invitational, University of
            Wisconsin-River Falls
1997   *18 American Potters Exhibition*, Moegi
            Gallery, Mashiko, Japan

John Neely

74 North 200 East
Logan, Utah 84321

Studio potter
Associate Professor, Ceramics Area Head, Assistant
Department Head, Graduate Program
    Chair, Utah State University

Travel:
Japan 1975, 1977-1980, 1982, 1993-1994, 1998

Education:
1975   B.F.A., New York State College of Ceramics
            at Alfred University
1975   Japan Foundation, One year Fellowship,
            Tokyo, Japan
1976   Rockefeller Brothers Fund, One year
            Fellowship, Tokyo, Japan
1982   M.F.A., Ceramics, Ohio University, Athens
            Japan Ministry of Education, two year Post
            Graduate Research Fellowship, Kyoto,
            Japan

Selected Exhibitions:
1990   *III World Triennial Exhibition of Small
            Ceramics*, Zagreb, Yugoslavia
            *The Fletcher Challenge Ceramics Award
            (1991, 1998)*, Auckland, New Zealand
1991   Solo Exhibition, Kyoto and Tokyo, Japan
1992   *Woodfire '92*, University of New England,
            Lismore, Australia
1993   *Muju International Clay Arts*, To-Art Space,
            Seoul, Korea
1996   *Yixing Western Potters Symposium
            Exhibition*, Yixing Factory Number Five,
            China
            Purple Sands T-Pots, Amsterdam,
            Netherlands
1998   Solo Exhibition, Casper College, WY

Selected Public Collections:
Bingham City Art Museum, UT
Ceramic Monthly, Columbus, OH
Everson Museum of Art, Syracuse, NY
The International Museum of Ceramic Art,
    New York State College of Ceramics at Alfred
New Mexico Junior College, Hobbs
Nora Eccles Harrison Museum of Art, Logan, Utah
The State University of New York College at
    Buffalo
University Museum, Southern Illinois University at
    Carbondale
Frederick R. Weisman Art Museum, Minneapolis,
    MN

Hiroshi Ogawa

1264 Wells Road
Elkton, Oregon 97436

Studio potter

Education:
1963   B.A., University of California, Santa
            Barbara
1964   Graduate studies, University of California,
            Santa Barbara
1965   Graduate studies, California State

University, Long Beach
1970-71 Ryukoku University, Kyoto, Japan
1970-72 Studied under Ken Azuma, Osaka, Japan

Travel:
Japan 1970-1972, 1986

Selected Exhibitions:
1972 Group Show, Osaka Midosuji Exhibition
Hall, Japan
1983 *Two Potters*, Umpqua Valley Arts Center,
Roseburg, OR
Juried Competition Exhibit, Coos Art
Museum, Coos Bay, OR
1985 *Crafts Invitational*, Coos Art Museum,
Coos Bay, OR
1986 *Earthly Meditations*, Umpqua Valley Arts
Center, Roseburg, OR
Pacific Vista, Clark College, Vancouver, WA
1990 *Two-person Show*, Umpqua Valley Arts
Center, Roseburg, OR
1991 *Umpqua Potters*, Umpqua Valley Arts
Center, Roseburg, OR
1997 *Hikarigama*, Umpqua Valley Arts Center,
Roseburg, OR

Don Reitz

P.O. Box 206
Clarkdale, Arizona 86324

Studio potter
Professor Emeritus, University of Wisconsin-
Madison

Education:
1957 B.S., Art Education, Kutztown State College,
PA
1962 M.F.A., New York State College of Ceramics
at Alfred University

Selected Exhibitions:
1986-88 *Craft Today: Poetry of the Physical*,
traveling exhibition, American Craft
Museum, New York, NY
1986 *Clay Az Art, International Ceramic
Conference*, Arabia, Finland
Palo Alto Cultural Center, CA
Large Vessels, Northern Illinois University
at DeKalb
1988 *100 Years of Wisconsin Art*, Milwaukee
Art Museum, WI
1990 *International Exhibition of Ceramics*,

Hovikodden Art Center, Oslo, Norway
Sculpture Centre Goesteatelier Hollufgaar,
Odense, Denmark
1991 Exhibition Culturele Raad Gemeentchuis,
Roden, Holland
American Woodfire '91, University of
Iowa, Iowa City
Nora Eccles Harrison Museum of Art,
Logan, Utah

Selected Public Collections:
The Arkansas Arts Center, Little Rock
The Art Institute of Chicago, IL
Evanston Art Center, IL
Fort Wayne Museum of Art, IN
High Museum of Art, Atlanta, GA
Los Angeles County Museum of Art, CA
Charles H. MacNider Museum, Mason City, IA
Milwaukee Museum of Art, WI
Museum of Contemporary Crafts, New York, NY
Renwick Gallery of the National Museum of
American Art, Smithsonian Institution,
Washington, DC

Mary Roehm

P.O. Box 430
New Paltz, New York 12561

Studio potter
Professor of Art, Ceramics, State University of
New York College at New Paltz

Education:
1973 B.F.A., Ceramics/sculpture, Daemen
College, Buffalo, NY
1979 M.F.A., Ceramics, Rochester Institute of
Technology, School of American Crafts,
NY

Travel:
China, Korea, Japan 1996, 1998

Selected Exhibitions:
1983 *Language of Clay*, Burchfield Art Center,
Buffalo, NY
1984 *Art for the Table*, American Craft Museum,
New York, NY
1986 *Poetry of the Physical*, American Craft
Museum, New York, NY
1987 *Clay in Space*, Fashion Institute of
Technology, New York, NY
1988 *Columnar*, Hudson River Museum, New

York, NY
Solo Exhibition, Pewabic Pottery, Detroit,
MI
1990 *Fragile Blossom, Enduring Earth: The
Japanese Influence on American
Ceramics*, American Craft Museum,
New York, NY
1991 *American Woodfire '91*, University of Iowa,
Iowa City
1994 *Solo Exhibition*, College Art Gallery, State
University of New York College at New
Paltz
1996 *Recent Guest Artist's Work*, The Shigaraki
Ceramic Cultural Park Museum, Japan

Selected Public Collections:
American Craft Museum, New York, NY
The Arkansas Arts Center, Little Rock
Brockton Art Museum, MA
Charles A. Wustum Museum of Art, Racine,
Wisconsin
The Detroit Institute of Arts, MI
Everson Museum of Art, Syracuse, NY
Phoenix Museum of Art, AZ
Renwick Gallery of the National Museum of
American Art, Smithsonian Institution,
Washington, DC
Shigaraki Ceramic Cultural Park Museum, Japan

Will Ruggles and
Douglass Rankin

Route 2, Box 235
Bakersville, North Carolina 28705

Studio potters

Education:
Will Ruggles:
1973-75 Grand Valley State Colleges, Allendale, MI
1975 Dung Chau University, Taipei, Taiwan
Chiang Mai University, Thailand
1977-78 Randy Johnston Pottery, River Falls, WI
1978 Workshop with Tatsuzo Shimaoka, Banff
Center for the Arts, Alberta, Canada
1992 Workshop with Warren MacKenzie,
Penland School of Crafts, NC

Douglass Rankin:
1971 B.A., Botany, Duke University, Durham,
NC
1975-76 Scholarship student, Penland School of
Crafts, NC

1976-78 Randy Johnston Pottery, River Falls, WI
1978 Workshop with Tatsuzo Shimaoka, Banff Center for the Arts, Alberta, Canada
1992 Workshop with Warren MacKenzie, Penland School of Crafts, NC

Selected Exhibitions:
1993 *Functional Ceramics 1993*, Wayne Center for the Arts, Wooster, OH
1994 *The Potters Art: Form and Function*, South Florida Art Center, Miami Beach
Rock Creek Pottery, Focus Gallery, Folkart Center, Asheville, NC
1997 *Alabama Clay Conference 12*, Jacksonville State University
Common Borders, Clemson University, SC
Nineteen American Potters, Moegi Gallery, Mashiko, Japan
1998 *28th Annual Ceramics Invitational: Wood Fired Ceramics*, University of Wisconsin-Whitewater
A Woman's Woodfire Invitational, Andrews University, Berrien Springs, MI
Ceramics Southeast, University of Georgia, Athens

Selected Public Collections:
Midwest Museum of American Art, Elkhart, IN
North Carolina Museum of History, Raleigh
Edward Orton Junior Ceramic Foundation

Jeff Shapiro

62 Raycliff Drive
Accord, New York 12404

Studio potter

Education:
1973-80 Work/study in Kyoto, Fukuoka, Ehime, Hamasaka and Bizen, Japan

Travel:
Japan

Selected Exhibitions:
1990 Toyoike Gallery, Japan
1991 Gallery Koko, Tokyo, Japan
1993 Takashimaya Department Store, Tokyo
1995 Takashimaya Department Store, Tokyo
1996 Matsuzakaya Department Store, Nagoya, Japan
1997 Tenmaya Department Store Gallery, Okayama, Japan

Selected Public Collections:
The Arkansas Arts Center, Little Rock
The Brooklyn Museum, NY
Everson Museum of Art, Syracuse, NY
Boca Raton Museum of Art, FL
Long House Foundation, East Hampton, NY

Mark Shapiro

Stonepool Pottery
Conwell Road
Worthington, Massachusetts 01098

Studio potter

Education:
1978 B.A., Anthropology, Amherst College, MA
1987 Penland School of Crafts, NC, Studio assistant to Mary Roehm
1989 Penland School of Crafts, NC, Studio assistant to Michael Simon

Selected Exhibitions:
1991 *American Woodfire '91*, University of Iowa Museum of Art, Iowa City
The Tea Party, American Craft Museum, New York, NY
1992 *Nine Massachusetts Potters*, Fitchburg Museum of Art, MA
1993 *NCECA Clay National*, San Diego Museum of Art, CA
1994 *Home and Garden*, Pewabic Pottery, Detroit, MI
1995 *Philadelphia Museum of Art Craft Show*, PA
1997 *Functional Work: American Potters*, Arvada Center for the Arts & Humanities, CO

Jane Shellenbarger

7654 West Esmond Road
Hale, Michigan 48739

Studio potter

Education:
1993 B.F.A., Kansas City Art Institute, MO
1996 M.F.A., Southern Illinois University at Edwardsville

Selected Exhibitions:
1995 *Clay Cup V*, Southern Illinois University, Carbondale
1996 *Images and Pots Clay Invitational*,

University of Wisconsin, River Falls
Rendezvous, Museum of Nebraska Art, Kearney
46th Annual Quad-State Juried Exhibition, Quincy Art Center, IL
1997 *Ceramic Forms*, Ronald Barr Gallery, Indiana University Southeast, Pontiac, MI
Archie Bray Foundation for the Ceramic Arts Exhibition, NCECA, Las Vegas, NV
Wood-fired Ceramic Exhibition, College of the Ozarks, Point Lookout, MO
Farewell Exhibition of Pottery, Archie Bray Foundation for the Ceramic Art, Helena, MT
1998 *Tea Bowl Invitational*, San Francisco Craft & Folk Art Museum, CA

Selected Public Collections:
Renwick Gallery of the National Museum of American Art, Smithsonian Institution, Washington, DC
The Archie Bray Foundation, Helena, MT
Southern Illinois University at Edwardsville

John Skelton

1530 South Sixth Street, Apt C-1010
Minneapolis, Minnesota 55454

Studio potter

Education:
1995 B.A., Mercer College, Macon, GA
1998 M.F.A., Ceramics, University of Minnesota, Minneapolis

Selected Exhibitions:
1996 *All-Purpose Show*, Katherine E. Nash Gallery, University of Minnesota, Minneapolis
1997 *Thaw: Annual Graduate Exhibition*, Katherine E. Nash Gallery, University of Minnesota, Minneapolis
1998 *Clay Bodies by Student Bodies*, Gustavus Adolphus Gallery, Gustus Adolphus, St. Peter, MN
Knobs, Katherine E. Nash Gallery, University of Minnesota, Minneapolis
M.F.A. Thesis Exhibition, Katherine E. Nash Gallery, University of Minnesota, Minneapolis

Byron Temple

P.O. Box 7914
Louisville, Kentucky 40257

Studio potter

Education:
    Ball State University
    Brooklyn Museum School, NY
    School of The Art Institute of Chicago, IL
1959-61 Apprenticed to Bernard Leach, St. Ives,
    England

Travel:
Spain, Japan, New Zealand, Australia, Netherlands

Selected Exhibitions:
1986 *Craft Today: Poetry of the Physical*,
    American Craft Museum, New York, NY
    Solo Exhibition, University of California,
    San Diego
1991 *American Woodfire '91*, University of Iowa
    Museum of Art, Iowa City
1992 *Solo Exhibition*, Indianapolis Museum of
    Art, IN
1994 Solo Exhibition, Ceramic ART, Sydney,
    Australia
1995 Solo Exhibition, Boymans-van Beuningen,
    Rotterdam, Netherlands
    Ceramic Kentucky, Society of Arts & Crafts,
    Boston, MA
1996 *Scripps Annual*, Scripps College, Claremont,
    CA
1997 *Two-person Exhibition*, Granberger
    Collection, Stockholm, Sweden
    Master Potters of the Heartland, Depauw
    University, Greencastle, IN

Selected Public Collections:
Museum Boymans-van Beuningen, Rotterdam,
    Netherlands
New Jersey State Museum, Trenton
Nora Eccles Harrison Museum of Art, Logan, UT
Kunstindustrimuseeum, Copenhagen, Denmark
Everson Museum of Art, Syracuse, NY
The Newark Museum, NJ
Nelson Museum, Arizona State University, Tempe
Rhode Island School of Design, Providence
Cooper-Hewitt National Design Museum,
    Smithsonian Institution, New York, NY
Taipei Fine Arts Museum, Republic of China

Skeff Thomas

15 Pindale Drive
Bridgeton, New Jersey 08302

Studio potter
Assistant Professor, Rowan University, Glassboro,
NJ

Education:
1986 B.A., Lewis and Clark College, Portland,
    OR
1986-87 Apprentice to Toshiko Takaezu,
    Quakertown, NJ
1993 M.F.A., Southern Illinois University at
    Edwardsville

Selected Exhibitions:
1994 *Colorado Clay Exhibition 1994*, Foothills
    Arts Center, Golden, CO
1995 *Colorado Clay Exhibition 1995*, Foothills
    Arts Center, Golden, CO
    Monarch National Ceramic Competition,
    Kennedy-Douglass Center for the Arts,
    Florence, AL
1996 *Ceramics U.S.A.*, University of North Texas,
    Denton
1997 *NCECA Clay National*, Barrick Museum,
    University of Las Vegas, NV
    *American Ceramic Society: Centennial
    Exhibition*, University of Kansas,
    Lawrence
    Craft Forms, Wayne Art Center, Wayne, PA
    26th Juried Show, Allentown Art Museum,
    PA
    Colorado Clay 1997, Foothills Art Center,
    Golden, CO

Jack Troy

540 Shively Road
Huntingdon, Pennsylvania 16652

Studio potter
Part-time Assistant Professor of Art, Juniata
College, Huntingdon, PA

Education:
1961 B.S., West Chester State College, PA
1962 Philadelphia College of Art, PA
1965-66 Summer sessions, New York State
    College of Ceramics at Alfred
    University

1967 M.A., English and Art, Kent State
    University, OH

Travel:
China, Japan, Sweden, New Zealand, New South
Wales, Australia, England, Columbia

Selected Exhibitions:
1976 *Teapots and Thoughts*, Montana State
    University, Bozeman
1979 *Function-non-Function*, Towson State
    College, MD
1981 *Fire and Ashes*, Pittsburgh Center for the
    Arts, PA
1985 *41st Scripps College Invitational*,
    Claremont, CA
1988 *SIUE Clay National*, Southern Illinois
    University at Edwardsville
1990 *Ashen Beauty*, Corvalis Art Center, OR
1991 *American Woodfire '91*, Museum of Art,
    University of Iowa, Iowa City
1995 *Clay/Wood/Fire/Salt*, NCECA Clay
    National Exhibition, Contemporary
    Artifacts Gallery, Berea, KY
1997 *Heroes, Icons, History and Memory*,
    Dallas Museum of Art, TX
1998 Solo Exhibition, Ceramic ART, Sydney,
    Australia

Selected Public Collections:
Arizona State University, Tempe
Arrowmont School of Arts and Crafts, Gatlinburg,
    TN
Auckland Museum of Art, New Zealand
Delaware Art Museum, Wilmington
Fletcher Brownbilt Collection, Contemporary
    Ceramics, Auckland, New Zealand
Leningrad School of Arts and Industry, Russia
Renwick Gallery of the National Museum of
    American Art, Smithsonian Institution,
    Washington, DC
Shigaraki Ceramic Cultural Park, Japan
Utah State University Museum of Art, Logan
William Penn Museum, Harrisburg, PA

Robert Archambeau

continued from page 10

the end of a road surrounded by total forest. Because of the almost constant risk of forest fires, a woodfire kiln could only be fired in the winter, which is very difficult at minus 35 degrees Fahrenheit and a woodfiring crew would not be readily available. However, I do have an unusually large supply of native soft woods to burn."

Rob Barnard

continued from page 14

paint on it hoping to create your own unique painting, then it is certainly a waste of time and, importantly, trees. Ultimately, what separates the serious ceramics artist from the indifferent ceramics artist is not what they make - sculpture or pottery - or how they fire - electric or wood - but rather the desire and willingness to explore and discuss in his or her work the kind of issues of which Yagi spoke. As he said, "No matter how interesting the procedure might have been, a boring object is just a boring object."

Paul Chaleff

continued from page 20

feet across, these bowl forms feel too large for use by one person, too large even for one family. My vocabulary of forms in this series includes round, square and boat-shaped cauldrons, saw-toothed cogs, auger-shaped conical forms, drum-shaped forms, tall saw-toothed forms, and most recently, a series of block-like crucibles which refer to the making of tools in concept and make more use of the negative spaces in their form. Scale and mass are important considerations in this work as I believe art to be language, and I want this work to engage the viewer in a very physical way.

I believe my work explores some of the positive areas of emotion and inquiry that have always existed in human society. I would like my work to exist in this time continuum. At first the historical associations may cause the viewer to be seemingly familiar with, but unable to categorize the work. I try to question our concepts of function and beauty/perfection. The most common comment my work has received is, "I know I shouldn't like this, but I do." There are deliberate flaws incorporated into this work that can only be deciphered as ceramic in origin. Upon closer examination, while touching, sitting upon or holding onto these pieces, the clues become apparent and the viewer can start to make the correct assumptions."

DATE DUE

GAYLORD			PRINTED IN U.S.A.